TEEN LIFE™

FREQUENTLY ASKED QUESTIONS ABOUT

Online Romance

Ann
Boger

ROSEN
PUBLISHING®

New York

Published in 2007 by The Rosen Publishing Group, Inc.
29 East 21st Street, New York, NY 10010

First Edition

Library of Congress Cataloging-in-Publication Data

Boger, Ann.
Frequently asked questions about online romance / Ann Boger. — 1st ed.
p. cm. — (FAQ: teen life)
ISBN-13: 978-1-4042-1971-7
ISBN-10: 1-4042-1971-4
1. Online dating. 2. Interpersonal relations in adolescence—Computer network resources. 3. Internet and teenagers. 4. Internet—Safety measures. I. Title.
HQ801.82.B64 2007
646.7'702854678—dc22

2006033651

Manufactured in the United States of America

Contents

Introduction

How many hours a day do you spend online? According to the Kaiser Family Foundation, teenagers between the ages of fifteen and eighteen generally spend an average of 6.5 hours each day online, watching television, and/or playing video games. Much of this time is spent multitasking, which means that teens often listen to music, play video games, send instant messages (IMs), check e-mail, and visit chat rooms all while the television is on. If you are like most teens, this time is largely recreational. You might spend it sending e-mails, photos, and instant messages to friends, but teens also spend a great deal of their time online visiting chat rooms and community groups such as MySpace.com, a place where users create personal profiles and chat with other members who share similar likes and dislikes in music, entertainment, hobbies, and more. According to a 2005 article in *Business Week* magazine, MySpace.com has more than 40 million members. Other community groups, though none on the scale of users that MySpace.com can boast, include Buzznet.com, Buzz-Oven.com, Tagworld.com, and Facebook.com.

As an increasing number of people use the Internet with greater frequency, it is only natural that many connections (and even romances) are formed. Even though the Internet makes it simple to meet people and make connections, especially for

When it comes to dating, many choose to log on. A 2006 survey reports that 16 million Americans have used Internet dating and similar services to find romance.

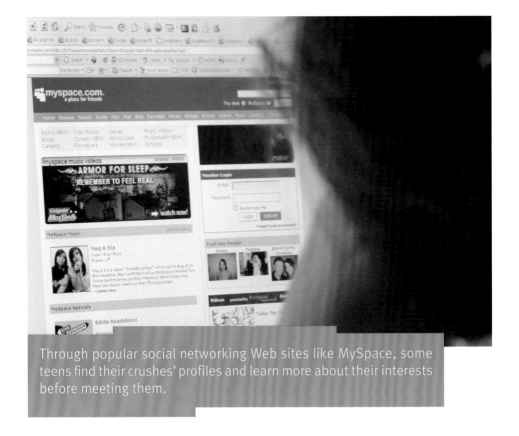

Through popular social networking Web sites like MySpace, some teens find their crushes' profiles and learn more about their interests before meeting them.

teens who are shy or who live in isolated towns and rural areas, it is not a replacement for meeting people in person. All people, especially teens, should learn good personal communication skills that they can use in social situations during school hours and in their everyday lives. Time spent on the Internet should never replace the social interactions that can come, for instance, from making eye contact at the library, asking someone for a dance at the winter formal, or striking up a conversation with someone you meet at the local sandwich shop. Even though social networking through the Internet is common and it has been going on with increasing frequency, it should never replace the social benefits of direct interaction with people.

Still, there are many advantages to finding friends online. You don't have to get dressed up, go out, or spend money. You're also assured, at least in the short run, that potential friends will form a first impression of you based on who you are (and what your beliefs, interests, and opinions are) as opposed to what your personal appearance is. If you're shy, the privacy and security of making conversation on a computer screen may make things easier for you. If you aren't interested or ready for a sexual relationship, you won't have the pressure of somebody making physical advances that you have to reject. And if you're gay, lesbian, bisexual, or questioning your sexuality, you can anonymously converse with others who question their sexuality without being forced "out of the closet." Even if you aren't ready for romance, meeting like-minded friends who are faced with the same confusion can be extremely comforting.

one

CAN YOU FIND LOVE ONLINE?

According to the Pew Internet & American Life Project, 87 percent of teens use the Internet. This means that there is an incredible wealth of Web sites, chat rooms, forums, e-zines, blogs, online books, advice columns, and bulletin boards designed and updated for people your age (often by teens themselves!). But aside from reading about other teens' good or bad online romances, what if you actually want to hook up with a virtual boyfriend or girlfriend of your own? How do you go about it? And how do you do it safely? For starters, there are a number of different approaches to meeting people online.

Discussion Groups

Discussion groups are a good place to begin forming social connections. Choose a subject that interests you, such as hiking, knitting, dancing, or photography and then search for Web sites that focus on your chosen topic. Many teen e-zines, online magazines, and Web sites host discussion groups concerning subjects that change daily. Getting involved in these discussions can be fun and can also put you in touch with others who share similar interests. Then, if you do decide that you like someone, it will be because both of you have expressed your feelings and opinions without a hidden romantic agenda.

Chat Rooms

Many Web sites feature chat rooms, which are a casual "drop-in" forum where people can come and go on a whim. Everyone in the chat room can read what you write and vice versa. If you're looking to meet people via a chat room, there are two ways to go about it. The first is to find and enter a chat room where the topics being discussed interest you. The second, more direct way is to find and enter a chat room that specifically caters to teen friend- ships, relationships, and romance. Chat rooms are often divided into various subcategories that specifically cater to teens seek- ing different experiences. For example, one chat room could be called "Potential Prom Dates" and another could be called "Seeking Skater Boys."

You might enter a chat room and discover that you seem to have nothing in common with the people there. You might find their conversations childish, stupid, aggressive, or offensive. If so, leave the chat right away and go to a different "room" where you feel more comfortable. Most chat rooms for teens have rules of conduct. These usually forbid using offensive or profane language and making hateful, sexist, or racist remarks, among other things. Most chat rooms also employ monitors that check in from time to time to ensure that nobody is breaking these rules. Chatters who act up or speak ill of others will be booted off and sometimes banned from the room.

Online Dating Networks and Social Services

If you're serious about wanting to meet somebody and don't want to waste time fishing around in discussion groups and chat rooms, you might want to try an online dating service. Although most of these are for adults, there are a few services that cater especially to teens, though most are geared toward users who are at least eighteen years old.

A more popular option for young people looking to meet new people (for both friendship and romance) is to use a social network site, such as Friendster.com or MySpace.com. Networking sites allow you to post a profile of yourself, including your likes and dislikes, hobbies, and photographs. Then, you can identify other posters as your friends (which will create a "friend list"). You will have to give permission each time someone wants to add you to his or her list of friends. Most sites include this policy as a safety feature so that your name doesn't appear on somebody's list unless you approve.

With so many people creating profiles and friends lists, these sites create a web—or social network—through which you can

Seventeen-year-old Katherine Lester, pictured with her father, Terry, made headlines in June of 2006 when she secretly flew to Israel to meet a twenty-five-year-old man she met on MySpace.

meet new people, especially friends of friends. You can view other people's profiles and friend lists; and, if you see someone that seems interesting, you can "approach" him or her by sending an instant message or e-mail. The person receiving the message has the option of whether or not to respond, protecting him or her (and you) from unwanted attention.

While social networks have quickly become one of the most popular choices for teens looking to increase their circle of friends, you should be extremely familiar with a Web site and how it works before you considering joining. Take some time to familiarize yourself with the site and its privacy policies. Fully read (and print out) any disclosure statements and/or site rules. Think about the rules of the site: Some sites only allow a defined community of users to read the content while others make public everything that users post, including photos and personal messages. Understand what sort of control you have over the information that you post and know that once you make information public that it cannot be retracted. When you choose a username, don't let it reveal too much about you, such as an indication of your hometown. Consider not posting your photo since it can be altered in ways you never intended. And finally, be sure that you would feel comfortable with anyone viewing the information that you are posting within the group since it might be there for years in the future. For instance, does your user "profile" contain any information that you wouldn't want your parents, siblings, friends, teachers, or supervisors viewing? Or does it contain any information or photos that could identify you or your high school, home address, phone number, or last

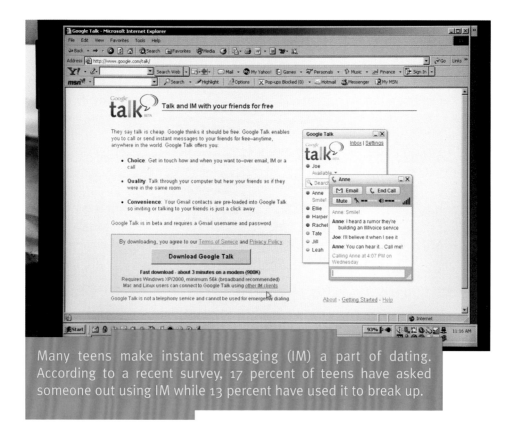

Many teens make instant messaging (IM) a part of dating. According to a recent survey, 17 percent of teens have asked someone out using IM while 13 percent have used it to break up.

name? If so, it might be impossible to remove such information once you publish it.

Private Chats and Instant Messaging

Most chat rooms are public "rooms" where you can interact with many people at the same time. If, however, you do happen to meet someone who interests you, all the conversations going on at the same room might seem chaotic or intrusive. If both of you agree, you and your new friend might want to head to a

10 FACTS ABOUT ONLINE ROMANCE

1 Nine out of ten teens use the Internet, and half of those do so on a daily basis.

2 Young people between the ages of eight and eighteen generally spend about one hour a day using the Internet for recreational use. For many teens, this means e-mailing and instant messaging friends and visiting chat rooms and other Web sites (such as MySpace.com) to make new ones.

3 Staying safe online is easy when you stay mysterious. Don't tell anyone your personal information, such as your telephone number or where you live or go to school.

4 The preferred form of communication among teens is instant messaging (IM), a fast and fun way to hold an online conversation in real time. This is a great way to stay in touch whether you live next door or across the globe, and it can be done anonymously with a username.

5 Social network Web sites, such as Friendster.com and MySpace.com are a very popular way to express yourself, share your creativity, and meet like-minded people. Before you begin using these networks, however, learn more about them, do some research, and read any disclaimers that appear on the Web sites themselves.

6 While the Internet can be a great place to make new friends and start a romance, not everyone you meet will be worth your while, and some will even be dangerous. Remember, people may not be who they claim to be online.

7 Between 12 and 24 percent of teens will take an online relationship offline and in person.

8 The first step in taking a relationship offline is to talk on the phone, and this should only be done after you have discussed doing so with your parents. Your phone number can tell someone a lot about you, including where you live.

9 Never go alone when meeting someone for the first time, and do not ride in a car or go to someone's house. Instead, pick a public place, take a good friend along, and always have a plan for how to safely end the meeting.

10 As long as you know the risks and proceed with caution, finding love on the Internet, or at least a good friend, is a very real possibility.

"private room" for a one-on-one conversation to get to know one another better.

Most chat services, which are often referred to as instant messaging (IM) services, offer you the option of going into a private chat room where you and your "guests" can chat among yourselves without outsiders. This can make getting closer a lot easier. Don't let yourself get too intimate, however. Remember that even though there are no longer twenty strangers milling around, the person you are talking with is still as unknown to you as he or she was in the public chat room. If the conversation takes a turn for the weird and you feel uncomfortable, don't think twice about saying good-bye and logging off.

E-mail

While not as immediate as IM, e-mail is a great way to communicate with friends. Exchanging e-mail addresses with someone you have recently met (either in person or online) allows you to share with them your thoughts and opinions—and to learn theirs—at your own pace. Not only can you send text via e-mails, you can also send photos (scanned or digital), voices and music (recorded), and even videos as attachments. The most important thing is that your e-mail address does not reveal too much personal information such as your first and last names.

two

HOW DO YOU STAY SAFE IN CYBERSPACE?

While the Internet can be a great place to make new friends, not everyone you meet will be worth your while and some people will even be dangerous. Remember, people are not always who they claim to be online. Some people lie about their age, appearance, income, occupation, and even gender! You can never really fully know a person unless you meet him or her in person. Teens who use the Internet to meet people should be as cautious as possible.

In 2006, five teenage boys in Los Angeles created a false profile of a fifteen-year-old girl on MySpace.com. The boys became concerned when a forty-eight-year-old man became interested in the "girl" and set a date to meet with her in a public park. Recognizing that this man could be dangerous, the boys called the police. Officers from the Federal Bureau of

In March 2006, Michael Ramos of Fontana, California, tried to lure a fifteen-year-old girl he met online into having sex. The girl, though, was fictitious, having been created by pranksters.

Investigation (FBI) later arrested the man for attempting to have sex with a minor. Luckily, in this instance, no one was hurt, but many other teens have been pressured into sex after developing an online relationship, and some who have refused have been harassed or even stalked.

Presenting Yourself Online

The latest software makes designing your own Web site fun. Social network Web sites make it very easy to post information about yourself online. Having your very own presence on the Internet is a great way to express yourself.

But there is a flip side. Remember that anyone can stumble onto your Web site, a place where perfect strangers can find out things about you and your life. Do not give out personal information such as your telephone number, address, or which school you go to, and do not reveal personal details that you would not want a stranger to know. Be equally careful about providing any information about friends and family members. You must also be careful about the images that you post online. For instance, you should never include pictures of yourself in front of street signs, your home, or your school.

The Name Game

Before entering a chat room or developing a profile on a social network Web site, you will be asked to give a username. For safety purposes, there are certain things you should consider before dreaming up a username of your own. For instance, it is not a good idea to use any version of your actual name. It is also a wise idea to keep it neutral. Teens who want to log on as "Hotdude" or "Sexymama" are obviously not looking for simple romance. Even if you think that you are just being flirtatious, choosing these kinds of names will work against you by attracting lots of unwanted attention. If you are female, you may want to pick a gender-neutral username so that your gender is concealed when you are in a chat room or newsgroup, but remember that Internet stalkers are equally likely to target young men as they are young women.

Once you have chosen the perfect username, never offer your real name to anyone you meet in a chat room, even when communicating with him or her in IMs or e-mails. Staying anonymous not only gives you an air of romantic mystery, it also protects your identity.

Just because a chat room or social network is for teens only doesn't mean that you'll find only teens in these rooms. After all, when you enter a room, there's no bouncer asking for ID to prove that you are eighteen years old or younger. As such, how do you really know that the charmer you're talking with is fifteen and not fifty-four?

Unfortunately, the fact that chat rooms are devoted to romance and are full of (relatively) inexperienced teens makes them very inviting for stalkers and pedophiles on the prowl for unknowing victims. You must remember that you never really know with whom you're sharing a conversation. Although this is useful for guarding your privacy and not giving away your identity

23 people here

Holly 18f Girl
Sxkaliber
FTLKelly
CRA1G 1103
Biglefty2
Easy Teen Girl

double click on name for more

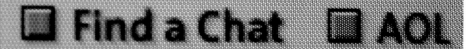 Find a Chat  AOL

Private Chat Noti

In Florida, the Law Enforcement Against Child Harm Task Force (LEACH) works to prevent Internet child exploitation. Pictured is a typical chat room LEACH uses to catch pedophiles online.

(in terms of being recognizable), it also means that you have no way of knowing whether the seemingly friendly and harmless person to whom you are communicating is telling the truth, lying, or doing a little bit of both. It is for this reason that you should follow these safety tips, particularly in the beginning stages of online relationships.

- Never reveal your real name, address, phone or fax number, social security number, where you work or go to school, or any other important information about you or anyone close to you (such as family and friends).
- Don't believe everything you read online. In many cases, people are lying or misrepresenting themselves.
- Don't telephone anyone who gives you his or her phone number. Even if it's an 800 number, caller ID allows the person to trace your call.
- Don't reveal any personal truths about yourself.
- Use good judgement when posting photos on the Internet, and don't send any of yourself (or anyone close to you, such as a boyfriend or girlfriend) to someone you don't know.
- If for any reason you sense that the person you're chatting with is acting strangely, being inconsistent, asking too many personal questions, or flat-out lying, trust your instincts: Make a polite excuse to get offline and say good-bye.
- If you are worried or scared about someone you met online or about a conversation that you had on your computer, tell your parents or a trusted adult immediately.

Sending and Receiving E-mail

When you open an e-mail account, you will be given or choose a password that allows you and only you to access your mail. Of course, if you give your password to someone else or use a ridiculously obvious one such as your middle name or the name of your favorite band, anybody can hack into your account and read your mail, even from another computer.

Electronic mail may feel like a private, secure form of communication. You type in a password to access your e-mail, you send messages only to certain people, and you delete those messages after you have read them, but e-mail is not really private. To maintain your privacy over e-mail, pick an e-mail address and username that do not reveal your real name or any other personal information about you.

If you decide to open e-mail accounts with services such as Yahoo.com or Hotmail.com, make sure you always completely sign out after accessing your mailbox. If you exit without doing so, the next person on the computer can read your correspondence as well—even if he or she doesn't know your password.

A Romantic Way of Communicating

If you have chatted for a few weeks or months with a cyberchum and you feel like you are really hitting it off, you might decide that you would like to exchange e-mail addresses so that you can write to each other outside of the chat rooms. One of the nicest things about making friends online is that you often have little messages and e-cards waiting for you in your mailbox when you return home from school or work. (There are many great Web sites with free "cards" that you can send to a friend or crush.) Writing e-mail, especially in this high-tech age, can be romantic, even old-fashioned like writing love letters in the days before telephones and mass transportation. Many people also find that it's easier to express their thoughts when given some time to compose a letter rather than having a face-to-face conversation.

You wouldn't want to dash off e-mail too quickly, however. Remember that the person receiving the message can read it again and again. Proofread your message again before you hit the send button. Are you being clear? Did you check for errors? Since you want to make the best impression, look it over and note the tone of your message. It's very easy for e-mail messages to be misunderstood. Unlike expressing yourself in a face-to-face meeting where you can read someone's facial expressions and body language, or a phone call where you can hear a person's tone of voice, e-mail is a flat message that is open to interpretation, especially in the earliest stages of a relationship. To avoid miscommunication, try to reread the message considering the receiver's point of view or frame of reference.

three

WHAT ARE SOME DANGERS TO AVOID?

The Internet can be a great tool for meeting people and making friends, but some people take things a little too far by suggesting that you immediately exchange telephone numbers or even engage in virtual cybersex. Either choice is not recommended. While adults have been known to explore the idea of making playful sexual advances in a virtual way, these activities can lead to potentially dangerous situations. You never want to suggest that you are open to sexual activities when you are not. Also, keep in mind that many chat rooms, especially those designed for teen use, will ban users from engaging in sexual role-playing and flirtations that offer the suggestion of sexual activities. Be aware that real sexual predators exist online and many of them are disguising themselves as young people with the hope of engaging teens in sexual discussions and activities. If you

Harold Spector of Beverly, Massachusetts, is arrested at Marshfield Municipal Airport on March 30, 2006. He was charged with allegedly seeking sex from a minor he met online.

are drawn into a sexual conversation, drop out of the mix and log off.

Many teens are actually attracted to sex discussions online simply because it allows them to explore their sexuality while remaining completely anonymous. Teens who tend to be more curious and less sexually experienced might be especially attracted to these experiences. While sexual activities are discouraged, cybersex is safer than engaging in actual sex. After all, there is no risk of getting pregnant, catching a sexually transmitted disease (STD), or being physically assaulted. However, if you think that cybersex is risk free, you are mistaken.

Cyberstalkers

In interviews, cyberstalkers often claim that they have fallen in love with their victims. Once they do so, they become obsessed

Lt. Paul O'Connell, who works at the Broward County Sheriff's Office in Florida, is part of the LEACH Task Force, which boasts a 98 percent conviction rate.

In April 1997, fifteen-year-old Billy Tamai of Emeryville, Canada, came forward as "Sommy," the cyberstalker who harassed his family and eluded authorities for several months.

and will stop at nothing in order to come into real-life contact with that person. If you think the fact that these stalkers can't see you and don't know your real name or whereabouts makes you safe, think again.

There are programs that can be downloaded for free from the Internet that allow people to make a "scan" of all the people in a chat room. In doing so, a person can figure out your ISP address and calculate your rough geographic location. Other programs allow a stalker to trace your computer's ID number. Once this is done, he or she can enter and use your computer as if you yourself were using it. Fortunately, this can be done only if you install one of these programs onto your computer. For this reason, never install any program you've never heard of onto your machine and use care whenever you decide to download anything.

Cyberstalkers are everywhere, but mostly in chat rooms and social network Web sites. And teens, with their combined sexual

Michael Torchia, Sangamon County adult probation director, poses with Cyber Sentinel, software designed to track the online activities of sex offenders on probation.

Myths and Facts

About Online Dating

Myth **Socializing online is for the emotionally unbalanced, dorks, and computer geeks who can't make friends the normal way.** Fact ➡ Socializing online is a standard practice among most American teens. In a national survey, 87 percent of teens reported using the Internet, and 75 percent of those teens use IM to communicate with friends. Of all teen groups, teen girls between the ages of fifteen and seventeen years old are most likely to be online.

Myth **It's safe for me to give personal information to someone I met on a social network Web site such as MySpace.com because they are listed as a friend of someone I actually know in real life.** Fact ➡ While new safeguards are developed frequently, it is never safe to give out your personal information on the Internet. It is not safe to assume that someone is who he or she claims to be, even if he or she claims to know one of your friends. Always be very careful not to share personal information, such as your telephone number or where you live or go to school, with anyone online. And, if you do decide to move beyond an online relationship, proceed with caution and discuss your plans with your parents beforehand.

 Only girls need to worry about sexual predators on the Internet. Fact ➥ Male and female teens are victimized by sexual offenders, and sexual offenders can be both men and women. A national survey found that 1 in 3 teen victims of online sexual solicitation were teen boys.

interest and inexperience, are targets. Some of these stalkers might come on to you right away. Others might be more indirect. They might appear understanding and subtly coax you to confide in them. They may pretend to be someone else or give you a sad story to gain your sympathy. Without your realizing it, they can discover your vulnerable points. They might even try to increase your confidence in them by subtly turning you against your parents and other people close to you with seemingly sympathetic advice. Although it might seem hard to believe that this could happen while you're in the comfort of your room, it happens all the time.

If you feel you are being stalked or harassed, try to copy down everything that appears in the "header" section of the message. Give this information to the sender's ISP (Internet service provider) when you contact it with a complaint. You should show the offensive e-mail to your parents or another adult. You and your parents can, and should, get in touch with your local or state police, the FBI, or the National Center for Missing and Exploited Children if any of the following online events have occurred:

- If you received any pornography (downloading child pornography is a federal crime)
- If you are propositioned by any adult who knows you are younger than eighteen
- If you received sexually explicit images created by someone who knows you are a minor
- If you or anyone you know is threatened or harassed

All of the above situations are considered crimes. It is important to remember that even though the criminal can't be seen and the crime is taking place via a computer, most Internet crimes are handled like crimes in the real world. It is also important to remember that being a victim of such crimes in no way means you were at fault or will be blamed.

Addiction

Addiction to the Internet is serious. It has led to failure at school, depression, broken friendships and relationships, and even lost jobs and broken marriages. Ultimately, no matter how exciting your online relationships might seem, they are neither real nor complete. The minute you log off, you are alone.

In August 2005, a mother shakes hands with Professor Tao Hongkai at a summer camp for Internet-addicted children in Beijing, China. Over 2 million Chinese youths have an Internet addiction.

How can you tell how much is too much? When your (or your parents') phone bills soar; when surfing gets in the way of schoolwork, jobs, social activities, and family responsibilities; when you're up all night and exhausted the next day; when your online relationships become more important than your real-life relationships—all of these are definite warning signs that you are dangerously hooked.

If you or your parents feel that you are spending too much time online, there are several options. One is to strictly limit the time you spend on the computer. Another is to get time-limiting or filtering software that restricts the time you spend online or the types of sites you can visit. Filtering software blocks sites that use certain keywords, such as "sex." Still another option is to get rid of your computer altogether (you can always use the one at school or at the library for homework and essays). Serious addicts should consider addiction counselling.

four

WHAT HAPPENS AFTER YOU'VE STARTED AN ONLINE ROMANCE?

Once you have met someone interesting online and something definitely clicks between you, where do you go from there? In some ways, beginning an online relationship is much the same as beginning an offline relationship. You start off by talking, asking questions, and getting to know each other. It is possible to grow to like someone you've never met or even talked to on the phone, especially since there is real power in being able to communicate over long periods about your likes and dislikes, similar personal experiences and histories, and shared hopes and dreams.

Many people debate the possibility of love at first sight. Attraction, desire, even infatuation—that's one thing. But is it possible to really fall in love with someone the moment you set eyes on him or her? Most people say that it's impossible to truly love someone without knowing the person first. Of course, online romances rule out love at first sight. But is there such a thing as love at first write? Can two people meet online and, after exchanging a few e-mails, fall head over heels?

Is Someone, Anyone Out There?

There are many needy, lonely, and even emotionally unbalanced people out there for whom the Internet is an important emotional outlet. Although many happy and healthy people chat, make friends, and even begin romances over the Internet, there are some people who project their needs, desires, and frustrations onto the people they meet online. Keep this in mind when getting to know prospective friends. Listen to your instincts when someone's writing makes you feel uncomfortable. It is better to be considered rude than an easy target.

There's No Need to Rush

Many people do find love online. But just as in real life, it's a bad idea to rush into things. Romances have a future only if both people have taken the time to get to know one another, to learn more about each other, and then to make sure that both are looking for the same things from a romantic relationship.

A particularly wise approach is to first concentrate on establishing a solid friendship. If things continue well and you both find that your feelings are deepening, you might want to take

Having a romantic online chat is much different than talking face-to-face or over the phone, but IM and e-mail allow you to vividly express yourself through writing.

the friendship a step further. There are no set rules for when and how to cross the bridge from being friends to being linked romantically. Making the proper decision is a matter of instinct, feeling things out, listening to each other, and trusting that your feelings are in sync.

The Language of Romance

Relating to people on the Internet can have obvious limitations, especially considering that you cannot hear the tone in someone's voice, see the look in his or her eyes, or read his or her body language. While relating to people over the Internet, the written word is all you've got. Luckily, there is a wide range of emotion icons ("emoticons") that can come in handy as potential romantic icebreakers.

Signs and Symbols

Here are some of the emoticons most commonly used in cyberspace: Emoticons are made by typing punctuation marks on the keyboard to make a "punctuation picture." Some e-mail providers, such as yahoo.com, also provide small images that can be inserted into e-mails.

Flirting online can be a fun and safe way to show let someone know that you are interested in him or her. Many young people find IM and private chats to be a good forum for making connections, and emoticons are a particularly fun and flirty way to communicate.

By using emoticons and online shorthand, you can react instantaneously and express a range of emotions with just a few keystrokes.

;-)	A wink (great for flirting or being sarcastic)
:-}	Embarrassed smile
:-(	A frown (means you're feeling down or have hurt feelings)
:'-(	Crying
:-D	Laughing/grinning
:-P	Sticking out your tongue
%-)	Confusion
:-x	Your lips are sealed
:-O	Surprise
0:)	You're an angel
>:->	You're a devil
@---<--	A rose
:-*	A kiss
{}	Putting someone's name inside the brackets means that you are giving that person a big hug. The more brackets, the tighter the hug. For example, {{{{{{Johnny}}}}}} would mean a very big hug.

Online Shorthand

Even more common than emoticons are abbreviations, also known as online shorthand. If you're in the middle of pouring out your heart, it can be time consuming to type out every word in full. So, many people resort to using shorthand. The following are some popular shorthand expressions:

2U2	To you, too
AFK	Away from keyboard
ASAP	As soon as possible
BAK	Back at keyboard
BBL	Be back later
BRB	Be right back
BTW	By the way
C4N	Ciao for now
CU	See you
CUL(8R)	See you later
CYA	See ya
DIY	Do it yourself
EOD	End of discussion
EZ	Easy
F2F	Face to face
FAQ	Frequently asked questions
FOAF	Friend of a friend

FOCL	Falling off chair laughing
FWIW	For what it's worth
FYI	For your information
GA	Go ahead
GAL	Get a life
GBTW	Get back to work
GFETE	Grinning from ear to ear
GR8	Great
GTG	Got to go
HAND	Have a nice day
HHOK	Ha ha only kidding
H/O	Hold on
IAC	In any case
IAE	In any event
IC	I see
IDGI	I don't get it
IMHO	In my humble opinion
IMO	In my opinion
IMPE	In my personal experience
IOW	In other words

Webcams capture voices, facial expressions, and body language, simulating the experience of directly talking to the person you're communicating with on the Internet.

IRL	In real life
IYKWIM	If you know what I mean
JIC	Just in case
J/K	Just kidding
KISS	Keep it simple stupid
L8TR	Later
LOL	Laughing out loud

LTNS	Long time no see
LYL	Love you lots
NRN	No reply necessary
ONNA	Oh no, not again!
OIC	Oh I see
OTF	On the floor
OLL	Online love
PLS	Please
PU	That stinks!
ROTF	Rolling on the floor
ROTFL	Rolling on the floor laughing
RSN	Real soon now
RUOK	Are you OK?
SH	Same here
SNAFU	Situation normal; all fouled up
TAFN	That's all for now
TEOTWAWKI	The end of the world as we know it
THX	Thanks
TIA	Thanks in advance
TLK2UL8R	Talk to you later

TSWC	Tell someone who cares
TTFN	Ta ta for now
TTYL(8R)	Talk to you later
TXS	Thanks
WB	Welcome back
w/	With
w/o	Without
WTG	Way to go
WU?	What's up?
ZZZ	Sleeping

Netiquette

Knowing how to behave online is known as "netiquette." Being polite and considering how others feel is just as important on the Internet as it is in person. Remember that what you say and how you say it, as well as how you act, will give other users—including potential crushes—their strongest impression of your character, your integrity, and who you are.

Good Netiquette	Poor Netiquette
You're polite and courteous online.	You swear, bully, and harass people, or make racist or sexist remarks banned from chat rooms (all of which can lead to the closure of your e-mail account and criminal charges).
Your e-mails are funny and original.	Your e-mails are full of spelling mistakes and incomplete sentences.
You always respond quickly to e-mails.	You take your sweet time responding to e-mails.
You politely join in on conversations when it is clear that you are welcome.	You always try to break in on other people's conversations.
In the middle of a conversation, you exit a chat room, disconnect, leave your computer, or sign off by saying good-bye.	In the middle of a conversation, you exit a chat room, disconnect, leave your computer, or sign off without any warning.

Ending the Online Romance

Immediately end a relationship if someone makes you uncomfortable, if he or she asks you to do something you do not want to do, or if he or she harasses you. In these situations, worry first about yourself and second about hurting someone's feelings or being rude.

If, on the other hand, at some point you realize that your online romance is not going anywhere, that you live too far away from each other for things to ever truly work out, that you just want to be friends, or that you're falling for someone else, don't end your online relationship by just dropping out of sight. Just as in real life, the least you owe someone is a sensitive good-bye with a bit of an explanation. After all, it isn't the other person's fault that he or she doesn't live up to your expectations.

CHAPTER five

HOW DO YOU STAY SAFE OFFLINE?

Some people might be perfectly content to never actually meet the friends they make online, while a few might desire the opportunity to meet in person. Maybe you just want to have a bit of fun, occasionally meeting friends in a chat room. Or perhaps you want to maintain a sort of ongoing pen-pal relationship with a slightly romantic edge. Of course, if it turns out that both of you live in different parts of the country, or even different parts of the world, you are probably limited to keeping your relationship online (unless you can afford the expensive cost of transportation or long-distance telephone bills).

In general, however, if you both find that your feelings are growing stronger and that your romance is developing, it is only natural that you will begin to think about eventually getting together in person.

Taking the Next Step

Although you shouldn't force a meeting before both of you are ready, if you do think things are getting serious, consider getting together. Know that the longer you wait, however, the more you risk investing a lot of feelings in a relationship that could be a potential letdown for one or both of you if things don't work out. Because of these and similar dangers, until you have actually met in real life, it is much wiser and safer to consider your companion as more of a close and special friend than a love interest.

Warning Signs

Carrying on an Internet romance has certain potential difficulties and dangers. Both stem from the fact that all you have to go on is someone's written word. Although some people are sincere and honest, others are not. Until you have met face-to-face, how can you be certain that a person has been completely honest with you?

Someone who makes excuses about why he or she can't meet with you is suspicious. One obvious reason is that the person is already involved in a relationship with someone else or is not who he or she claimed to be. If you feel that someone is being too evasive, confront him or her and demand the truth.

At the same time, be wary of someone who pressures you into meeting face-to-face before you are ready. It is essential that you feel safe—and take precautions—when meeting someone in person for the first time.

Ten Great Questions to Ask Yourself About Online Romance

1 In which chat rooms and Web sites are you most likely to find other teens with similar interests?

2 Is your username, Web site, or profile safely crafted so as not to reveal any private or personal information?

3 Do you trust this person well enough to give him or her your e-mail address?

4 If you receive any suspicious e-mail, is it spam or harassment?

5 What will you do if someone makes you uncomfortable?

6 Are you spending too much time online?

7 Are you ready to take your relationship offline?

8 Is it OK for you to take your online romance to next level by exchanging phone numbers?

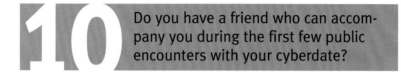

9 How safe is your plan for the first offline meeting?

10 Do you have a friend who can accompany you during the first few public encounters with your cyberdate?

How to Be Sure

How can you be sure when—or even if—you should meet offline? There is no real answer to this question. For the most part, you have to go with your instincts. Do you care about each other? Do you feel comfortable with each other? Do you trust each other? Do you feel ready to take your relationship a step further? If you answered yes to all of these questions, the timing is probably right to get together face-to-face.

The Phone Call

For many reasons—particularly safety—your first offline contact should be over the telephone. You can often tell a lot about someone by his or her voice. Before exchanging phone numbers, however, ask permission to do so from your parents by discussing your desire to share personal information with a friend you don't know well. Giving out your phone number to someone you haven't actually met is a big deal. If you, or your parents, feel funny about it, tell your friend that you'll call him or her (and

Being Web smart and savvy makes online romance safe and fun. In fact, a 2006 survey states that 52 percent of Internet daters described their experiences as mostly positive.

then do so from a pay phone—just in case he or she has caller ID, which traces the numbers of incoming phone calls).

The First Meeting

Chances are that the excitement, nervousness, and anticipation you experienced before your first phone conversation will be nothing compared to that which precedes your first face-to-face encounter. In spite of—and because of—these feelings, you should take the following precautions when planning the meeting:

▶ Do not go alone. It's best to bring a few friends along. Although it might not be so romantic, it's safer. Plus, a group outing can be even more fun. If your "mystery" friend brings one or two of his or her friends, too, you never know who might hit it off. If you can't find at least one person to go along with you, reschedule your first meeting.

▶ Plan to meet in a public place (such as a diner, a mall, a party, a football game, or a concert). And no matter how well the meeting goes or how trustworthy your friend seems, stay in a public place. Don't let your guard down or agree to go to a place that is secluded or private.

▶ Let your parents know what you're up to, where you're going, and what time you'll be home. Make sure that they also have all of your friend's information including his or her name, phone number, and address.

➤ Plan to make your first meeting brief. That way, you can easily remove yourself if you decide your date wasn't what you were expecting, or if you begin to feel uncomfortable for any reason.

➤ Don't let your date pick you up or drive you home. Being alone with each other in the car could lead to you being the target of a robbery or a rape, and you may not want the person to know where you live just yet.

➤ Do not drink any alcohol or do any drugs. At best, because of your already nervous state, drugs and alcohol might make you say things you'll later regret. At worst, they could lead to your date taking advantage of you in any number of dangerous ways.

➤ During your date, don't leave your belongings unattended if you go to the bathroom. Similarly, if you leave food or a drink unfinished when you get up, don't eat or drink when you come back. Although this might sound paranoid, there have been cases of first meetings in which seemingly nice and normal people slipped tranquilizers or other drugs into their date's food or drink.

➤ Always make sure that you have a cell phone or some spare change for a pay phone. That way, if you find yourself in an uncomfortable situation, help will be only a phone call away.

As the Internet continues to grow and more and more people worldwide become "connected," online relationships, whether romantic or not, will continue to thrive. The Internet is wonderful in that it can bring so many different kinds of people together. As long as you know the risks and proceed with caution, finding meaningful friendships and other relationships on the Internet is a very real possibility.

Glossary

browser A browser is a software program that allows you access to Web sites. Two of the most common browsers are Netscape Navigator and Internet Explorer. These can be purchased or downloaded directly from the Internet.

chat room A Web site that allows multiple users to enter a conversation in real time.

cyberstalker A person who repeatedly threatens or harasses another person online.

instant message (IM) A real-time text conversation similar to public and/or private chat rooms.

Internet A worldwide system of computers connected by one gigantic network. People whose computers are connected to this network can send information and communicate with each other.

modem Aside from a computer and a phone line, in order to log on to the Internet, you will need a device called a modem, which connects your computer to the Internet through your phone or cable line. Most modems come installed as part of your computer.

provider A provider, or Internet service provider (ISP), such as America Online or Earthlink, is a service that gives you access to the Internet. Most providers charge monthly fees for partial or unlimited use.

social network A Web site community such as Friendster.com or MySpace.com, where you can post a personal profile and meet others with similar interests or shared friends.

username An online code name.

Federal Bureau of Investigation
Office of Crimes Against Children
935 Pennsylvania Avenue NW, Room 4127
Washington, DC 20535
(202) 324-3000
Web site: http://www.fbi.gov/kids/kids.htm
It is the mission of the FBI's Crimes Against Children
(CAC) program to provide a quick and effective response
to all incidences of crimes against children. Making this a
priority increases the number of victimized teens safely
recovered and reduces the level of crime in which children
are targets.

Internet Keep Safe Coalition
Web site: http://www.iKeepSafe.org
iKeepSafe.org is a coalition of forty-nine governors, law
enforcement, the American Medical Association, the
American Academy of Pediatrics, and other associations
dedicated to helping parents, educators, and caregivers by
providing tools and guidelines to teach teens and children
the safe and healthy use of technology.

i-SAFE, Inc.
5900 Pasteur Court, Suite #100
Carlsbad, CA 92008
(760) 603-7911

Web site: http://www.isafe.org
  i-SAFE Inc. is the worldwide leader in Internet safety education.
  Founded in 1998 and endorsed by the U.S. Congress, i-SAFE
  is a non-profit foundation dedicated to protecting the online
  experiences of youth everywhere.

National Center for Missing & Exploited Children
Charles B. Wang International Children's Building
699 Prince Street
Alexandria, VA 22314-3175
(703) 274-3900
(800) THE-LOST (843-5678)
Web site: http://www.missingkids.com
  The National Center for Missing & Exploited Children's
  mission is to help prevent child abduction and sexual
  exploitation; help find missing children; and assist victims
  of child abduction and sexual exploitation, their families,
  and the professionals who serve them.

National Cyber Security Alliance
Web site: http://www.staysafeonline.org
  NCSA is a non-profit organization that provides tools and
  resources to empower home users; small businesses; and
  schools, colleges, and universities to stay safe online. A
  public-private partnership, NCSA members include the
  Department of Homeland Security, the Federal Trade
  Commission, and many private-sector corporations and
  organizations.

NetSmartz Workshop
Web site: http://www.netsmartz.org

The NetSmartz Workshop is an interactive, educational safety resource from the National Center for Missing & Exploited Children and Boys & Girls Clubs of America for children age five to seventeen, parents, guardians, educators, and law enforcement that uses age-appropriate, 3-D activities to teach children how to stay safer on the Internet.

On Guard Online Hotline
(877) FTC-HELP (382-4357)
Web site: http://www.onguardonline.gov
   The Federal Trade Commission manages OnGuardOnline.gov, which provides practical tips from the federal government and the technology industry to help you be on guard against Internet fraud, secure your computer, and protect your personal information.

Web Sites
Due to the changing nature of Internet links, Rosen Publishing has developed an online list of Web sites related to the subject of this book. This site is updated regularly. Please use this link to access the list:

http://www.rosenlinks.com/faq/onro

For Further Reading

Hatchell, Deborah. *What Smart Teenagers Need to Know...About Dating, Relationships, and Sex.* Santa Barbara, CA: Piper Books, 2003.

MacDonald, Joan Vos. *Cybersafety: Surfing Safely Online* (Teen Issues). Berkeley Heights, NJ: Enslow Publishers, 2001.

Packer, Alex. *The How Rude! Handbook of Friendship and Dating Manners for Teens: Surviving the Social Scene.* Minneapolis, MN: Free Spirit Publishing, 2003.

Rothman, Kevin F. *Coping with Dangers on the Internet: A Teen's Guide to Staying Safe Online.* New York, NY: Rosen Publishing Group, 2000.

Tarbox, Katherine. *Katie.com: My Story.* New York, NY: E. P. Dutton, 2000.

Finkelhor, D., Mitchell, K. J., and Wolak, J. "Highlights of
the Youth Internet Safety Survey." *Juvenile Justice Fact
Sheet* – FS200104. Washington, DC: US Government
Printing Office, pp. 1–2.

Hitlin, Paul. "Teens and Technology: Youth Are Leading the
Transition to a Fully Wired and Mobile Nation." Pew
Internet and American Life Project: Teens and
Technology. Retrieved June 5, 2006 (http://www.
pewinternet.org/PPF/r/162/report_display.asp).

Kaiser Family Foundation Press Release. "'Media Multi-
Tasking' Changing the Amount and Nature of Young
People's Media Use." Kaiser Family Foundation.
Retrieved June 5, 2006 (http://www.kff.org/entmedia/
entmedia030905nr.cfm).

National Cyber Security Alliance. "How to Talk to Young
People About Socializing Safely Online."
Staysafeonline.org. Retrieved June 5, 2006 (http://www.
staysafeonline.org/connectedandprotectededucators.html).

Wiredsafety.org. "Cyberdating: How to Have Fun But Stay
Safe." Wiredsafety.org. Retrieved June 5, 2006 (http://
www.wiredsafety.org/internet101/aromance.html).

Index

Photo Credits

Cover © www.istockphoto.com/Sladjan Lukic; p. 5 © www.istockphoto.com; p. 6 © Nicholas Kamm/AFP/Getty Images; p. 11 © Bill Pugliano/Getty Images; p. 13 © David Paul Morris/Getty Images; pp. 18, 26, 28, 29 © AP/Wide World Photos; pp. 21, 27 © Joe Raedle/Getty Images; p. 33 © Cancan Chu/Getty Images; p. 37 (left) © www.istockphoto.com/Nicholas Monu; p. 37 (right) © www.istockphoto.com/Mikhail Lavrenov; p. 39 © www.istockphoto.com/Willie B. Thomas; p. 43 © www.istockphoto.com/Manuel Velasco; p. 52 © www.istockphoto.com/Marcy Smith.

Designer: Evelyn Horovicz;
Photo Researcher: Tahara Anderson